Teach Like Ced™

Cultural Sentence Strips Literacy Framework

A Practical Guide to Teaching Literacy Through Structure, Voice, and SELF

Cedric A. Washington
Internationally Recognized Educator, Author, and Curriculum Designer

Who Lives Like This?! Publishing LLC
Griffith, Indiana
© 2025 Cedric A. Washington

Teach Like Ced™ Cultural Sentence Strips Literacy Framework
A Practical Guide to Teaching Literacy Through Structure, Voice, and SELF

© 2025 by **Cedric A. Washington**

All rights reserved.

No part of this publication may be reproduced, distributed, or transmitted in any form or by any means—electronic, mechanical, photocopying, recording, or otherwise—without the prior written permission of the publisher, except in the case of brief quotations embodied in critical reviews and certain other noncommercial uses permitted by copyright law.

Published by:
Who Lives Like This?! Publishing LLC
Indianapolis, Indiana
United States of America

Teach Like Ced™, **Cultural Sentence Strips Literacy Framework**, and **Knowledge of SELF™** are trademarks of Cedric A. Washington. Unauthorized use of these names, frameworks, or methodologies is prohibited.

This book is designed to support professional learning and instructional practice. It is not intended to replace district policies, state standards, or professional judgment, but to serve as a research-aligned framework for effective literacy instruction.

ISBN: 978-1-970680-15-7

Printed in the United States of America

About the Author

Cedric A. Washington is an **internationally recognized educator, author, curriculum designer, and speaker**, known for his unapologetic commitment to literacy, cultural intelligence, and student empowerment. He is the creator of the **Teach Like Ced™ Cultural Sentence Strips Literacy Framework** and the **Knowledge of SELF™ (Social Empowerment Learning Framework)**—innovative instructional systems designed to restore structure, clarity, and agency to education.

With more than two decades of experience in classrooms, mentoring programs, and professional development spaces, Washington has worked extensively with **educators, school districts, nonprofit organizations, and youth-serving institutions** across the United States and internationally. His work centers on one core belief:

> **Literacy is liberation when students are taught how to think, speak, and write with ownership.**

Washington is the author of *The MISEDUCATION of the Negro in the 21st Century*, a research-based memoir and educational text that examines identity, culture, power, and schooling in modern education systems. His writing and curricula are widely recognized for bridging academic rigor with cultural relevance—without controversy, dilution, or lowered expectations.

As the Founder and Executive Director of **NERD Youth Services, Inc.**, Washington has led mentoring, literacy, and leadership initiatives serving youth and families throughout Northwest Indiana and beyond. His work emphasizes long-term outcomes, intergenerational impact, and the development of confident, articulate thinkers.

Cedric A. Washington is also a former collegiate athlete whose background in sports deeply informs his instructional philosophy—particularly the importance of discipline, repetition, structure, and earned mastery. These principles are embedded throughout the Teach Like Ced™ framework.

Through keynote addresses, professional development, and curriculum adoption, Washington continues to influence educators globally, advocating for literacy instruction that honors culture, demands excellence, and prepares students not just for school—but for life.

SECTION I — THE PHILOSOPHY

Chapter 1 — Literacy as Liberation
Power, Identity, and Self-Definition Through Language

Chapter 2 — Why Writing Builds Reading
Writing as the Gateway to Comprehension and Thinking

Chapter 3 — SELF vs. Traditional SEL: Literacy, Identity, and Ownership
From Behavior Management to Intellectual Agency

Chapter 4 — Culture as Pedagogy: Teaching Without Controversy, Teaching With Truth
Cultural Intelligence as Instructional Precision

SECTION II — THE INSTRUCTIONAL MODEL

Chapter 5 — The Sentence → Paragraph → Essay Framework
How Writing Mastery Is Built Intentionally

Chapter 6 — The Monday–Friday Instructional Flow
Predictable Rhythm for Sustainable Literacy Growth

SECTION III — CLASSROOM PRACTICE

Chapter 7 — Using the Teacher's Edition With Fidelity and Professional Autonomy
Structure That Protects Equity and Expertise

Chapter 8 — Using the Student Workbook as a Cognitive Workspace
Writing as Daily Intellectual Practice

Chapter 9 — Time Management in the Literacy Block
Focused Instruction That Multiplies Impact

SECTION IV — ASSESSMENT & STUDENT GROWTH

Chapter 10 — Differentiation and Intervention Without Lowering the Ceiling
Access Without Reduction

Chapter 11 — Assessment for Growth, Not Punishment
Humanizing Accountability Through Writing

Chapter 12 — Oral Presentation, Student Voice, and Intellectual Confidence
Speaking as Proof of Ownership

SECTION V — FIDELITY & IMPACT

Chapter 13 — Fidelity, Integrity, and Long-Term Impact
Protecting the Framework. Sustaining Legacy.

APPENDICES

Appendix A — Research Alignment and Academic Foundations

Appendix B — Standards Crosswalk
Reading, Writing, Speaking & Listening

Appendix C — Sample Lesson Walkthrough
Sentence → Paragraph → Presentation

Appendix D — Family Engagement as Cultural Partnership

FOREWORD

Literacy instruction is at a crossroads.

Across classrooms, districts, and institutions, educators are working harder than ever—yet outcomes remain uneven. Students can decode words but struggle to explain ideas. They can complete assignments but lack confidence in their own thinking. Teachers are handed programs filled with activities, yet little clarity about *why* those activities matter or *how* mastery is built.

What is missing is not effort.
What is missing is **structure with purpose**.

Teach Like Ced™ Cultural Sentence Strips Literacy Framework enters this moment not as another trend, but as **a course correction**. It restores intentionality to literacy instruction by reconnecting three elements that were never meant to be separated: **culture, structure, and voice**.

This framework does not ask educators to abandon standards, rigor, or professionalism. It asks them to sharpen those commitments. It reminds us that literacy is not mastered through exposure alone, but through **explicit instruction, disciplined practice, and ownership of language**.

At its core, Teach Like Ced™ recognizes a simple truth:
Students think more clearly when they are taught *how* thinking is built.

By centering sentence-level clarity, honoring oral language as a cognitive asset, and sequencing writing instruction with precision, this framework provides educators with something rare in modern education—**a repeatable pathway to mastery**.

This is not a script.
This is not a shortcut.

It is a blueprint.

The pages that follow challenge educators to teach with intention, to protect instructional integrity, and to see literacy not as compliance, but as empowerment. They invite leaders to move beyond surface-level adoption toward fidelity-driven implementation. And most importantly, they affirm students as thinkers whose voices deserve structure, clarity, and respect.

Teach Like Ced™ is not about teaching louder.
It is about teaching **clearer**.

INTRODUCTION

Why Teach Like Ced™

Every educator remembers a student who "knew the answer" but could not explain it.

They could speak passionately in conversation yet froze when asked to write. They had ideas, opinions, and insight—but lacked the structure to organize those thoughts into sentences, paragraphs, and arguments that carried weight.

Too often, these students are mislabeled.

They are called struggling.
They are called disengaged.
They are called behind.

Teach Like Ced™ was created to challenge those labels.

This framework begins with a conviction grounded in both research and lived experience:

> **Most students do not struggle because they lack intelligence.**
> **They struggle because they were never taught how literacy is constructed.**

The Problem Teach Like Ced™ Solves

In many literacy classrooms today:
- Writing is assigned before it is taught
- Reading is assessed without explanation
- Culture is treated as an add-on rather than a foundation
- Voice is encouraged without structure

The result is predictable: frustration for students, burnout for teachers, and inconsistent outcomes across classrooms.

Teach Like Ced™ exists to restore **clarity**.

What Makes Teach Like Ced™ Different

Teach Like Ced™ is built on five core commitments:

1. **Structure Is Non-Negotiable**
Students deserve explicit instruction that shows how ideas are built—not vague expectations.
2. **Writing Is the Engine of Literacy**
Writing reveals understanding, accelerates reading comprehension, and builds confidence.
3. **Culture Is Pedagogy**
Students' language patterns, experiences, and oral traditions are assets—not obstacles.

4. **Voice Requires Discipline**
Expression without clarity limits power. Structure sharpens voice.
5. **Fidelity Protects Equity**
When instruction is consistent and intentional, all students gain access to mastery.

Why Sentence Strips Matter

Sentence strips are not elementary tools.

They are **thinking tools**.

When students learn to:
- Construct clear sentences
- Explain reasoning
- Revise for meaning

They gain control over language, and with it, confidence.

Sentence-level mastery is the gateway to paragraph development, essay writing, oral presentation, and critical thinking.

Who This Framework Is For

Teach Like Ced™ is designed for:
- Classroom teachers (elementary through secondary)
- Literacy coaches and instructional leaders
- Tutors and after-school educators
- District curriculum teams
- Teacher preparation programs

The framework is adaptable across settings while remaining structurally intact.

What This Book Will Do

This book will:
- Explain the *why* behind effective literacy instruction
- Show the *how* through practical models
- Protect the *integrity* of the framework as it scales

It is written to be studied, implemented, and revisited—not skimmed.

A Final Word to the Educator

Teaching literacy is not about covering material.

It is about **building thinkers**.

Teach Like Ced™ invites you to teach with clarity, to honor culture without compromise, and to trust that when students are given structure, they rise to meet it.

This is not just a framework.
It is a stance.

SECTION I

THE PHILOSOPHY

Literacy is not neutral.
It is power, agency, and self-definition.

This section establishes the intellectual foundation of Teach Like Ced™. It explores literacy as liberation, the relationship between writing and reading, the limitations of traditional SEL, and the role of culture as pedagogy. These chapters explain **why structure, voice, and SELF must exist together** for literacy instruction to be transformative.

CHAPTER 1

Literacy as Liberation

Teach Like Ced™ Educator Handbook

Cedric A. Washington
Who Lives Like This?! Publishing LLC

Introduction: Literacy Is Never Neutral

Literacy has never been neutral.

It has never simply been about reading books, passing tests, or mastering grammar rules. Literacy has always been about **power**—who holds it, who is denied it, and who learns to navigate systems because they can read, write, and reason within them.

To teach literacy as if it is neutral is to ignore history.
To teach literacy without cultural awareness is to misunderstand how children learn.
To teach literacy without voice is to train compliance, not thinking.

Teach Like Ced™ begins with a foundational truth:

> **Literacy is liberation when it is taught with intention, structure, and cultural intelligence.**
>
> This chapter establishes why literacy must be taught not merely as a skill set, but as a **tool for agency, self-definition, and intellectual empowerment.**

The Historical Context: Why Literacy Has Always Been Controlled

Throughout history, access to literacy has been strategically restricted.

In the United States:
- Enslaved Isrealites were legally prohibited from learning to read or write.
- Literacy was criminalized because it enabled organization, resistance, and self-determination.
- Education for marginalized communities was often intentionally underfunded, fragmented, or stripped of rigor.

These realities were not accidental. They were rooted in the understanding that **a literate population cannot be easily controlled**.

Literacy allows individuals to:
- Interpret laws rather than merely obey them
- Question narratives rather than accept them
- Write their own stories rather than live inside someone else's

Teach Like Ced™ recognizes that when students struggle with literacy today, the issue is rarely intelligence. More often, it is **instructional design divorced from cultural reality**.

The Modern Miseducation: Skills Without Power

In contemporary classrooms, literacy instruction often looks polished but hollow.

Students are taught:
- How to identify the main idea
- How to circle keywords
- How to select the "best" answer

But they are rarely taught:
- How to develop an idea
- How to defend a position
- How to articulate their thinking clearly and confidently

This creates what Teach Like Ced™ identifies as **functional literacy without agency**.

Students may read words, but they cannot:
- Explain *why* something matters
- Argue *how* ideas connect
- Express *who* they are as thinkers

This is miseducation—not because content is missing, but because **purpose is missing**.

Writing as the Gateway to Thinking

Teach Like Ced™ asserts that writing is not the final product of literacy—it is the **gateway**.

When students write, they are forced to confront their thinking honestly. Writing exposes:
- Confusion
- Gaps in reasoning
- Weak understanding
- Strengths that oral discussion may hide

A student who cannot write a clear sentence does not yet fully understand their idea. This is not a deficit—it is a diagnostic reality.

Teach Like Ced™ treats writing as:
- A thinking tool
- A comprehension check
- A pathway to intellectual confidence

Rather than asking students to prove understanding through tests alone, Teach Like Ced™ centers writing as **evidence of cognition**.

Culture as the Foundation of Literacy Development

Children do not enter classrooms as blank slates.

They arrive with:
- Language patterns learned at home
- Storytelling traditions rooted in community
- Cultural norms around communication, expression, and reasoning

To pretend that culture does not influence literacy is to misunderstand human development.

Teach Like Ced™ defines culture as:

The shared language, experiences, values, and meaning-making systems that shape how students interpret the world.

Culture is not an add-on.
Culture is the **starting point**.

When instruction ignores culture, students are forced to translate before they can learn. When instruction honors culture, students can **transfer existing strengths into academic language**.

From Oral Tradition to Written Mastery

Long before formal schooling, cultures across the world relied on oral tradition to transmit:
- History
- Morality
- Knowledge
- Identity

Teach Like Ced™ recognizes oral language as a **legitimate intellectual asset**, not a distraction from "real learning."

Students who can:
- Speak passionately
- Explain verbally
- Debate informally

already possess the foundation for strong writing.

The task of the educator is not to erase this ability, but to **refine and structure it**.

Teach Like Ced™ bridges oral language and written expression by:
- Encouraging students to speak about ideas before writing
- Using sentence frames to translate speech into academic form
- Teaching students that their voice matters—and can be sharpened

Literacy and Self-Definition

At its core, literacy is about **self-definition**.

Students who lack literacy are often defined by:
- Test scores
- Labels
- Assumptions

Students who possess literacy can:
- Define themselves
- Explain their choices
- Advocate for their needs
- Challenge misrepresentation

Teach Like Ced™ connects literacy directly to identity through the SELF framework, ensuring that students do not just write sentences—but write **positions**.

A student who writes:

"I believe education matters because it creates opportunity."

is beginning the work of self-definition.

Teach Like Ced™ pushes further by asking:
- *What kind of opportunity?*
- *For whom?*
- *Who decides?*

This is literacy as liberation in action.

What Literacy as Liberation Looks Like in the Classroom

In Teach Like Ced™ classrooms:
- Writing is daily, structured, and purposeful
- Student voice is honored and refined, not silenced
- Cultural references are used to clarify learning, not politicize it
- Structure provides safety, not restriction

Students are not asked merely to respond.
They are asked to **reason**.

Teachers are not asked to improvise.
They are asked to **execute with intention**.

What Literacy as Liberation Is Not

To maintain clarity and fidelity, it is essential to define what Teach Like Ced™ does **not** represent.

Literacy as liberation is not:
- Political indoctrination
- Ideological instruction
- Lowering academic expectations
- Centering feelings over thinking

Instead, it is:
- Structured
- Disciplined
- Rigorous
- Human-centered

Conclusion: The Responsibility of the Educator

Educators do more than teach standards.

They shape how students see:
- Knowledge
- Themselves
- Their place in the world

Teach Like Ced™ calls educators to recognize that literacy instruction is a moral act. It determines whether students become:
- Passive recipients of information

or
- Active constructors of meaning

Literacy as liberation is not optional.
It is **necessary**.

This chapter lays the foundation.

The chapters that follow will show **how** this philosophy becomes daily practice.

CHAPTER 2

Why Writing Builds Reading

Teach Like Ced™ Educator Handbook

Cedric A. Washington
Who Lives Like This?! Publishing LLC

Introduction: The Literacy Lie We've Been Taught

For decades, literacy instruction has been built on a false hierarchy:

First, students learn to read. Then—once they are ready"—they learn to write.

This belief has shaped curricula, pacing guides, assessments, and interventions across the country. It sounds logical. It feels intuitive. And it is fundamentally flawed.

Teach Like Ced™ rejects this separation.

Reading and writing are not sequential skills.
They are **reciprocal cognitive processes**.

You do not truly read unless you can reconstruct meaning.
You do not truly understand unless you can articulate thought.

This chapter establishes a core Teach Like Ced™ principle:

Writing does not follow reading. Writing reveals reading.

The Cognitive Relationship Between Reading and Writing

Reading is often taught as consumption.
Writing is often taught as production.

In reality, both are acts of **construction**.

When students read, they must:
- Decode symbols
- Interpret meaning
- Connect ideas
- Evaluate intent

When students write, they must:
- Organize thoughts
- Clarify meaning
- Select vocabulary

- Anticipate audience

Writing **forces** the same cognitive work that strong reading requires—only more transparently.

Teach Like Ced™ recognizes writing as the most honest window into a student's comprehension. Multiple-choice answers can mask misunderstanding. Writing cannot.

Why Writing Exposes Understanding Faster Than Tests

A student may correctly answer a comprehension question without truly understanding the text. This happens because:
- Answer choices cue responses
- Context eliminates wrong options
- Test-taking strategies compensate for gaps

Writing removes these crutches.

When a student is asked to write:
- A single sentence explaining a text
- A short paragraph defending a claim
- A response connecting ideas

Their thinking becomes visible.

Teach Like Ced™ positions writing as:
- A formative assessment tool
- A diagnostic instrument
- A growth tracker

Not because writing is harder—but because it is **more honest**.

The Sentence as the Smallest Unit of Comprehension

In Teach Like Ced™, the sentence is sacred.

Why?

Because a sentence requires:
- A complete thought
- Logical coherence
- Purposeful word choice

A student who cannot write a complete sentence does not yet fully understand their idea. This is not a judgment—it is a signal.

Teach Like Ced™ uses sentence-level writing to:

- Check comprehension immediately
- Prevent gaps from compounding
- Build confidence incrementally

Before students summarize passages, analyze themes, or write essays, they must be able to write **one clear sentence that makes sense**.

Writing Forces Precision Where Reading Can Remain Vague

Students can often "get the gist" of a text without understanding it deeply.

Writing demands precision.

When students write, they must decide:
- What matters most
- What words best convey meaning
- How ideas connect

This decision-making process strengthens reading because students begin to read with intention:
- Looking for evidence
- Noticing structure
- Attending to language

Teach Like Ced™ students read differently because they know they will have to **say something meaningful afterward**.

Writing as Active Reading

Teach Like Ced™ reframes writing as **active reading**.

Instead of asking students to:
- Highlight passages aimlessly
- Answer disconnected questions

Students are asked to:
- Write about what they read
- Explain their reasoning
- Defend interpretations

This shifts students from passive receivers of text to **active constructors of meaning**.

Why Struggling Readers Often Improve Through Writing

Traditional intervention for struggling readers often focuses exclusively on reading skills:

- Phonics drills
- Fluency passages
- Isolated comprehension strategies

While these have value, they often fail to address the underlying issue: **students do not know how to organize and express thought**.

Teach Like Ced™ uses writing to support struggling readers by:
- Slowing thinking down
- Making comprehension visible
- Reducing cognitive overload through structure

When students write short, structured responses:
- They focus on one idea at a time
- They gain clarity
- They experience success

Success builds confidence.
Confidence fuels engagement.
Engagement accelerates growth.

Oral Language as the Bridge Between Reading and Writing

Teach Like Ced™ does not ask students to write in isolation.

Before students write, they:
- Talk
- Explain
- Rehearse ideas aloud

Oral language acts as a bridge between reading and writing by:
- Clarifying thinking
- Reducing anxiety
- Allowing immediate feedback

Students often know what they want to say but struggle to write it. Speaking helps them **find the words**.

Teach Like Ced™ honors oral language as:
- A cognitive rehearsal space
- A cultural strength
- A literacy accelerator

From Sentence to Meaning: A Classroom Example

A student reads a short passage.

Instead of asking:

"What is the main idea?"

Teach Like Ced™ asks:

"Write one sentence explaining what the author wants us to understand."

The teacher models:
- How to form a claim
- How to use evidence
- How to clarify language

Students write.
Teachers read responses.
Understanding is revealed immediately.

This is writing building reading in real time.

Why Writing Builds Vocabulary Better Than Memorization

Vocabulary lists teach definitions.
Writing teaches **application**.

When students write using new vocabulary:
- Words move from passive recognition to active use
- Meaning becomes contextual
- Retention increases

Teach Like Ced™ embeds vocabulary into writing because:
- Words stick when they are used purposefully
- Students learn how language works, not just what it means

The Equity Implication of Writing-Centered Literacy

Students from language-rich homes often gain early exposure to:
- Argument
- Explanation
- Storytelling

Students from under-resourced environments may not receive the same academic language exposure—not because of lack of intelligence, but because of access.

Teach Like Ced™ levels the playing field by:
- Teaching language explicitly
- Providing sentence frames
- Modeling academic expression

Writing becomes a tool of **access**, not gatekeeping.

What Writing-Builds-Reading Is Not

To maintain clarity, Teach Like Ced™ defines what this approach is not.

It is not:
- Excessive journaling without feedback
- Creative writing without structure
- Writing used only for grading

It is:
- Intentional
- Structured
- Aligned to comprehension
- Used daily, not occasionally

The Educator's Role in Writing-Centered Literacy

Educators must shift their mindset.

Writing is not something students do after instruction.
Writing **is** instruction.

Teachers who embrace this shift:
- Catch misunderstandings early
- Teach more effectively
- Empower students faster

Teach Like Ced™ equips educators to use writing as a **thinking amplifier**, not a punishment or afterthought.

Conclusion: Writing as the Key to Mastery

Teach Like Ced™ asserts that literacy mastery is impossible without writing.

Writing:
- Sharpens thinking
- Strengthens reading
- Builds confidence
- Reveals understanding

When students write well, they read with purpose.
When they read with purpose, learning accelerates.

This chapter establishes why writing sits at the center of the Teach Like Ced™ framework.

The next chapter will explore how writing must be paired with **SELF**—so literacy does not merely produce skilled students, but **self-aware, self-governing thinkers**.

CHAPTER 3

SELF vs. Traditional SEL: Literacy, Identity, and Ownership

Teach Like Ced™ Educator Handbook

Cedric A. Washington
Who Lives Like This?! Publishing LLC

Introduction: The Limits of Teaching Behavior Without Teaching Being

Over the last decade, Social-Emotional Learning (SEL) has become a dominant force in education. Districts have adopted frameworks, purchased programs, and trained educators to focus on student emotions, behaviors, and interpersonal skills.

The intention is admirable.
The execution, however, is often incomplete.

Teach Like Ced™ does not reject SEL.
It **extends it**.

This chapter introduces **SELF (Social Empowerment Learning Framework)** as a necessary evolution—one that moves beyond emotional regulation into **identity, reasoning, ownership, and agency**, all of which are essential to meaningful literacy development.

The central argument of this chapter is clear:

> **Students cannot fully own their writing, reading, or thinking until they own themselves.**

What Traditional SEL Gets Right—and Where It Stops Short

Traditional SEL frameworks typically emphasize:
- Self-awareness
- Self-management
- Social awareness
- Relationship skills
- Responsible decision-making

These competencies are important. They help students navigate emotions, relationships, and classroom expectations.

However, in practice, SEL is often reduced to:
- Behavior management
- Emotional check-ins
- Compliance-oriented regulation

Students are frequently asked:
- *How do you feel?*
- *Did you follow expectations?*
- *What strategy can you use to calm down?*

While these questions matter, they stop short of the deeper work.

Teach Like Ced™ identifies the gap:

Traditional SEL manages behavior.
It does not always develop **identity or ownership**.

The Problem With Emotional Literacy Alone

Emotional awareness without intellectual empowerment can unintentionally produce passivity.

Students may learn:
- How to calm themselves
- How to follow rules
- How to articulate feelings

But they may never learn:
- Why they think the way they do
- How their experiences shape interpretation
- How to assert ideas respectfully
- How to challenge narratives with evidence

In literacy instruction, this gap is especially harmful.

A student who can say:

"I feel frustrated"

but cannot say:

"I disagree with this idea because…"

has emotional vocabulary without **intellectual voice**.

Teach Like Ced™ exists to close that gap.

Introducing SELF: Social Empowerment Learning Framework

SELF is not a behavior program.
SELF is an **identity and agency framework**.

Teach Like Ced™ embeds SELF directly into literacy instruction because language is the primary way identity is expressed, refined, and defended.

SELF is built on five interdependent pillars:
1. **SELF Conscience**
2. **SELF Governing**
3. **Social Conscience**
4. **Aspirations**
5. **Good People Skills**

Each pillar directly supports stronger reading, writing, speaking, and thinking.

SELF Conscience: Knowing Who You Are as a Thinker

SELF Conscience is the foundation.

It asks students to examine:
- Their beliefs
- Their reasoning
- Their perspective

In literacy, SELF Conscience shows up when students:
- Take ownership of their ideas
- Use "I believe" statements
- Reflect on how experiences shape interpretation

Teach Like Ced™ teaches students that **their thoughts matter**, but also that thoughts must be supported, refined, and communicated clearly.

Example:
Instead of correcting a student's opinion, the teacher asks:

"What makes you think that?"

This question moves students from expression to **reasoning**.

SELF Governing: Ownership Over Choices and Words

SELF Governing moves beyond rule-following.

It teaches students to:
- Monitor their thinking
- Revise their work intentionally
- Make choices based on purpose, not impulse

In writing, SELF Governing is practiced when students:
- Revise for clarity, not just correctness

- Decide which words best express meaning
- Accept feedback as growth, not punishment

Teach Like Ced™ reframes revision as **self-governance**, not teacher control.

Social Conscience: Understanding Audience and Impact

Writing is not written into a vacuum.

Social Conscience teaches students to consider:
- Audience
- Tone
- Impact of language

Students learn that:
- Words have consequences
- Clarity matters
- Respect strengthens communication

In Teach Like Ced™ classrooms, students are taught to:
- Disagree without disrespect
- Argue ideas, not people
- Communicate thoughtfully

This skill is essential for academic discourse and civic engagement.

Aspirations: Writing Toward the Future

Many students write as if their words disappear once graded.

Teach Like Ced™ reframes writing as a tool for **future-building**.

Aspirations encourage students to:
- Connect literacy to goals
- See writing as transferable power
- Understand how language opens doors

Students begin to see writing as:
- Preparation for careers
- Preparation for leadership
- Preparation for advocacy

When students understand *why* literacy matters, effort increases.

Good People Skills: Literacy as Relationship-Building

Good People Skills focus on:
- Listening
- Responding thoughtfully
- Collaborating respectfully

In literacy instruction, this appears through:
- Peer discussions
- Feedback conversations
- Oral presentations

Teach Like Ced™ teaches students that strong communicators are not just skilled—they are **considerate, aware, and intentional**.

Why SELF Must Be Integrated Into Literacy—Not Taught Separately

Many schools teach SEL in isolation:
- Morning meetings
- Advisory periods
- Separate lessons

Teach Like Ced™ integrates SELF into **daily literacy practice** because:
- Identity is developed through language
- Agency is practiced through expression
- Empowerment is reinforced through writing

Students do not learn SELF by talking about it.
They learn SELF by **using it**.

The Cultural Imperative of SELF

For students whose voices have historically been marginalized, SELF is not optional.

Students who are not taught to:
- Own their thinking
- Express ideas clearly
- Advocate through language

are often misunderstood, mislabeled, or underestimated.

Teach Like Ced™ ensures that literacy instruction does not strip students of identity in the name of "standardization."

Instead, it teaches students to **translate who they are into academic language**—a skill that preserves culture while expanding access.

What SELF Is Not

To protect fidelity, Teach Like Ced™ clearly defines what SELF is not.

SELF is not:
- Therapy
- Political ideology
- Emotional indulgence
- Replacement for academic rigor

SELF is:
- Structured
- Disciplined
- Integrated
- Academic

The Educator's Role in Teaching SELF Through Literacy

Educators are not asked to become counselors.

They are asked to:
- Ask better questions
- Model thinking aloud
- Honor student voice while demanding clarity
- Create space for reasoning, not just responses

Teach Like Ced™ equips educators to teach **whole students through language**, not around them.

Conclusion: Literacy With Ownership Changes Everything

Students who develop SELF do not write to please teachers.

They write to:
- Clarify ideas
- Defend positions
- Express identity
- Shape understanding

Literacy becomes an act of ownership, not obedience.

This chapter establishes why Teach Like Ced™ insists that literacy instruction must develop **thinkers with agency**, not just students with skills.

The next chapter will show how this philosophy is translated into **daily instructional structure**—where empowerment meets precision.

CHAPTER 4

Culture as Pedagogy: Teaching Without Controversy, Teaching With Truth

Teach Like Ced™ Educator Handbook

Cedric A. Washington
Who Lives Like This?! Publishing LLC

Introduction: Culture Is Not the Problem—It Is the Missing Link

One of the most persistent myths in education is that teaching should be "culture-free."

This belief is often framed as professionalism or neutrality, yet in practice it functions as something else entirely: **the elevation of one cultural norm while labeling all others as distractions**.

Teach Like Ced™ rejects this myth.

Culture is not an obstacle to learning.
Culture is **how learning happens**.

This chapter establishes a foundational truth:

> **All teaching is cultural. The question is whether we acknowledge it or ignore it.**

What Culture Actually Means in Education

Teach Like Ced™ defines culture broadly and precisely.

Culture is not:
- Political affiliation
- Ideological stance
- Demographic labels

Culture is:
- Language patterns
- Communication styles
- Ways of reasoning
- Storytelling traditions
- Norms around authority, dialogue, and expression

Every classroom already has a culture.
Ignoring it does not remove its influence, it simply **leaves it unexamined**.

The Hidden Curriculum of "Neutral" Instruction

So-called "neutral" instruction often privileges:
- Certain ways of speaking
- Certain ways of writing
- Certain ways of demonstrating understanding

Students who naturally align with these norms are labeled "advanced."
Students who do not are labeled "struggling."

Teach Like Ced™ identifies this as a **pedagogical blind spot**, not a student failure.

When instruction assumes a single cultural entry point, it unintentionally turns difference into deficiency.

Culture as the Entry Point, Not the Endpoint

Teach Like Ced™ does not romanticize culture, nor does it trap students within it.

Culture is used as:
- An entry point for comprehension
- A bridge to academic language
- A scaffold toward mastery

Students are not asked to abandon who they are.
They are taught how to **translate** who they are into academic contexts.

This is the difference between cultural relevance and cultural reduction.

Why Culturally Intelligent Teaching Accelerates Literacy

Students comprehend faster when:
- Examples resonate with lived experience
- Language patterns feel familiar
- Instruction connects to known frameworks

This is not lowering rigor.
This is **reducing cognitive distance**.

Teach Like Ced™ leverages cultural familiarity so students can devote cognitive energy to:
- Structure
- Vocabulary
- Reasoning
- Revision

When students no longer struggle to access meaning, they can focus on **mastery**

Oral Tradition as an Academic Asset

Many students come from communities where:
- Storytelling is central
- Verbal explanation is valued
- Call-and-response is natural

Traditional classrooms often interpret these strengths as:
- Disruptions
- Off-task behavior
- Lack of discipline

Teach Like Ced™ reframes oral tradition as:
- A literacy foundation
- A reasoning platform
- A pre-writing tool

Speaking becomes rehearsal.
Listening becomes discipline.
Dialogue becomes structure.

Teaching Academic Language Without Erasing Identity

Teach Like Ced™ is explicit about academic language.

Students are taught:
- How academic language works
- When it is required
- Why it carries power

This instruction is framed as **addition, not replacement**.

Students learn:

"You already know how to express ideas. Now let me show you how to express them in ways that open doors."

This preserves identity while expanding access.

Avoiding Controversy by Staying Grounded in Pedagogy

Teach Like Ced™ does not engage in political discourse.

The framework remains grounded in:
- Cognitive science
- Language development

- Instructional clarity

Culture is addressed as:
- A learning variable
- A communication system
- A cognitive resource

Not as:
- A political stance
- A social agenda
- A moral battleground

This is how Teach Like Ced™ remains **district-safe and classroom-true**.

What Culture as Pedagogy Looks Like in Practice

In Teach Like Ced™ classrooms:
- Teachers model academic language explicitly
- Students practice translating ideas into formal writing
- Examples reflect diverse lived experiences without stereotyping
- Structure remains non-negotiable

Students learn that:
- Their voice matters
- Clarity matters more
- Precision is power

Common Missteps in Culturally Responsive Instruction

Teach Like Ced™ avoids common pitfalls such as:
- Overemphasizing relevance at the expense of rigor
- Using culture as decoration rather than instruction
- Lowering expectations in the name of inclusion

True cultural pedagogy **raises the ceiling**.

The Equity Implication of Cultural Pedagogy

Equity is not achieved by treating all students the same.

Equity is achieved by:
- Teaching students how systems work
- Providing access to academic language
- Valuing diverse ways of knowing while demanding excellence

Teach Like Ced™ ensures that literacy instruction becomes a tool of access, not exclusion.

The Educator's Responsibility

Educators are cultural transmitters whether they acknowledge it or not.

Teach Like Ced™ asks educators to:
- Teach with awareness
- Lead with structure
- Honor voice without abandoning rigor

This is not extra work.
This is **better work**.

Conclusion: Truth Without Noise

Culture does not politicize education.
Ignoring culture does.

Teach Like Ced™ teaches educators to:
- Engage culture thoughtfully
- Teach literacy precisely
- Empower students responsibly

This chapter anchors the framework in truth—without controversy, without apology, and without confusion.

The next chapter transitions from philosophy to **daily instructional execution**, where culture, structure, and literacy meet practice.

SECTION II: THE INSTRUCTIONAL MODEL

CLASSROOM PRACTICE

Structure lives in execution.

This section translates philosophy and model into daily classroom practice. It clarifies how educators use the Teacher's Edition with fidelity, leverage the Student Workbook as a cognitive workspace, and manage time intentionally to protect literacy instruction.

CHAPTER 5

The Sentence → Paragraph → Essay Framework

Teach Like Ced™ Educator Handbook

Cedric A. Washington
Who Lives Like This?! Publishing LLC

Introduction: Why Most Writing Instruction Fails Students

Most students do not struggle with writing because they lack ideas.

They struggle because they were never taught **how ideas are constructed**.

In many classrooms, students are asked to:
- Write paragraphs before mastering sentences
- Write essays before understanding structure
- Express thoughts before learning how language works

Teach Like Ced™ identifies this as an instructional sequencing failure—not a student deficit.

This chapter establishes a core truth:

Writing mastery is developmental, not spontaneous.

Students must be taught how complexity is built.

Why Structure Is Not the Enemy of Creativity

One of the most common misconceptions in education is that structure limits creativity.

Teach Like Ced™ asserts the opposite.

Structure:
- Reduces anxiety
- Clarifies expectations
- Frees cognitive space for ideas

Creativity flourishes when students know:
- Where to start
- What is expected
- How to improve

Structure does not suppress voice.
It **amplifies it**.

The Sentence: The Smallest Unit of Thought

Teach Like Ced™ treats the sentence as the foundation of all writing.

A sentence requires:
- A clear idea
- Logical order
- Purposeful word choice

If a student cannot write a complete sentence that expresses a coherent idea, they are not yet ready for paragraphs or essays.

This is not punitive.
It is **developmentally sound**.

Teaching Sentences with Intention

In Teach Like Ced™, sentences are taught explicitly.

Students learn:
- What makes a sentence complete
- How to state a claim
- How to add reasoning
- How to clarify meaning

Example Sentence Frame:

I believe ___ because ___.

This frame teaches:
- Opinion ownership
- Reasoning
- Cause-and-effect thinking

Sentence frames are not crutches.
They are **training tools**.

Why Sentence-Level Mastery Changes Everything

When students master sentences:
- Writing confidence increases
- Reading comprehension improves
- Revision becomes manageable

Sentence-level mastery allows teachers to:
- Diagnose misunderstandings quickly

- Provide targeted feedback
- Prevent gaps from compounding

Teach Like Ced™ insists that **no student advances without sentence clarity**.

From Sentences to Paragraphs: Developing Ideas

Once students can write strong sentences, Teach Like Ced™ moves to paragraphs.

A paragraph is taught as:
- One idea
- Developed through multiple sentences
- Connected logically

Students learn that a paragraph is not a length requirement, it is a **thinking unit**.

Teaching Paragraph Structure Explicitly

Teach Like Ced™ teaches paragraph writing through:
- Topic sentences
- Supporting details
- Explanation
- Closing or transition

Students are shown how sentences work together.

Example Progression:
1. Claim sentence
2. Evidence or example
3. Explanation
4. Clarifying or concluding sentence

This structure builds coherence and depth.

Why Paragraph Instruction Is Critical

Without paragraph instruction:
- Essays become disorganized
- Ideas remain underdeveloped
- Students lose confidence

Teach Like Ced™ treats paragraph writing as **the bridge between thinking and argument**.

Paragraphs teach students how to:

- Stay on topic
- Expand ideas
- Build logic

From Paragraphs to Essays: Earning Complexity

Teach Like Ced™ does not rush students into essays.

Essays are introduced only when students can:
- Write clear paragraphs
- Maintain focus
- Develop ideas logically

An essay is taught as:
- A collection of connected paragraphs
- Unified by a central claim

Students learn that essays are not mysterious; they are **structured thinking at scale**.

Demystifying the Essay

Teach Like Ced™ removes fear from essay writing by:
- Breaking it into familiar parts
- Reusing sentence and paragraph structures
- Modeling thinking aloud

Students see that essays are:
- Expanded sentences
- Organized paragraphs
- Clear reasoning

This demystification empowers students.

Differentiation Within the Framework

The Sentence → Paragraph → Essay framework is inherently differentiated.

Teachers adjust:
- Sentence complexity
- Paragraph length
- Essay expectations

But the structure remains intact.

Struggling students receive:

- More modeling
- More rehearsal
- More scaffolding

Advanced students receive:
- Expanded sentence types
- Deeper analysis
- Greater independence

Common Missteps in Writing Instruction

Teach Like Ced™ avoids:
- Assigning essays without preparation
- Correcting mechanics before meaning
- Confusing length with quality

Structure comes before polish.
Clarity comes before correctness.

The Educator's Role in Structured Writing Instruction

Educators are not editors.
They are **architects of thought**.

Teach Like Ced™ asks educators to:
- Model writing openly
- Teach structure explicitly
- Demand clarity with compassion

This shifts writing instruction from frustration to empowerment.

Conclusion: Mastery Is Built, Not Discovered

The Sentence → Paragraph → Essay framework restores logic to literacy instruction.

Students are not overwhelmed.
Teachers are not guessing.
Progress is visible.

This framework ensures that writing instruction becomes:
- Intentional
- Equitable
- Empowering

The next chapter will show how this framework is executed within a **predictable weekly rhythm** that supports both teachers and students.

CHAPTER 6

The Monday–Friday Instructional Flow

Teach Like Ced™ Educator Handbook

Cedric A. Washington
Who Lives Like This?! Publishing LLC

Introduction: Why Rhythm Matters in Literacy Instruction

Students do not just learn content.
They learn **patterns**.

They learn when to listen.
They learn when to speak.
They learn when to try, revise, reflect, and perform.

One of the most overlooked elements in literacy instruction is **instructional rhythm**—the predictable flow that reduces anxiety, increases engagement, and creates psychological safety for learning.

Teach Like Ced™ is not rigid.
It is **reliably structured**.

This chapter introduces the Monday–Friday instructional flow that ensures literacy instruction is:
- Predictable without being boring
- Structured without being scripted
- Rigorous without being overwhelming

Why Predictability Is a Cognitive Asset

When students know what to expect, cognitive energy is freed for learning.

Predictable structure:
- Reduces behavioral issues
- Increases participation
- Improves task completion
- Builds confidence

Teach Like Ced™ recognizes that **uncertainty is exhausting**, especially for students who already navigate complex environments.

The weekly flow creates a learning environment where:
- Students feel safe to try
- Mistakes are expected
- Growth is visible

The Weekly Arc: From Input to Ownership

Teach Like Ced™ follows a clear instructional arc each week:
1. **Modeling**
2. **Guided Practice**
3. **Development**
4. **Refinement**
5. **Application**

This arc mirrors how humans learn complex skills—not how pacing guides are written.

Each day has a distinct purpose.
Each purpose builds toward mastery.

Monday: Modeling & Meaning-Making

Monday sets the tone.

This is where teachers:
- Introduce the focus skill
- Model thinking aloud
- Write in front of students

Teach Like Ced™ insists that teachers **show the work**, not just assign it.

What Happens on Monday:
- Teacher models sentence or paragraph construction
- Mistakes are made intentionally and corrected publicly
- Language choices are explained, not assumed

Students learn:
- How thinking becomes writing
- That confusion is part of the process
- That writing is constructed, not gifted

Monday is about **clarity**, not speed.

Tuesday: Oral Language & Guided Practice

Tuesday is where students begin to engage actively—but not independently yet.

Teach Like Ced™ recognizes that many students know what they want to say but struggle to write it.

Tuesday bridges that gap.

What Happens on Tuesday:
- Students rehearse ideas orally
- Sentence frames are practiced aloud
- Teachers coach language in real time

Oral rehearsal:
- Reduces writing anxiety
- Clarifies thinking
- Honors cultural communication styles

Tuesday ensures students **say it before they write it**.

Wednesday: Paragraph Development & Structured Writing

Wednesday is the pivot point.

Students move from supported practice to **structured independence**.

What Happens on Wednesday:
- Students write independently within clear structure
- Teachers circulate and confer
- Feedback focuses on clarity and meaning

This is not a test day.
This is a **development day**.

Students are encouraged to:
- Take risks
- Ask questions
- Revise in the moment

Thursday: Revision, Dialogue, and Deepening Thought

Thursday is where thinking sharpens.

Teach Like Ced™ treats revision as:
- An act of self-governance
- A sign of ownership
- A necessary literacy skill

What Happens on Thursday:

- Students revise for clarity, not just correctness
- Peer discussions focus on ideas
- Teachers guide reflection

Students learn that:
- First drafts are not failures
- Revision is power
- Clarity is earned

Thursday transforms writing from a task into a **craft**.

Friday: Application, Presentation, and Reflection

Friday is not a "fun day."
It is a **transfer day**.

Students apply what they've learned in new contexts.

What Happens on Friday:
- Students present ideas orally or in writing
- Learning is connected to real-world contexts
- Reflection solidifies growth

Reflection questions may include:
- What did I improve this week?
- What challenged me?
- How did my thinking change?

Friday builds **agency**.

Students leave the week knowing they grew.

Why This Flow Works Across Settings

The Monday–Friday flow is flexible by design.

It works in:
- Traditional classrooms
- Block schedules
- Tutoring programs
- After-school spaces
- Home learning environments

The structure remains intact even when time is adjusted.

Teach Like Ced™ is **portable pedagogy**.

Differentiation Within the Weekly Flow

Differentiation happens within the structure, not outside of it.

Teachers adjust:
- Amount of modeling
- Level of scaffolding
- Complexity of writing tasks

But the rhythm remains.

This consistency is what allows students of all levels to progress.

Common Mistakes in Weekly Planning

Teach Like Ced™ avoids:
- Treating every day the same
- Rushing to independence
- Skipping revision
- Using Friday as a reward day

Each day has instructional weight.

Skipping a day disrupts the arc.

The Educator's Role in the Weekly Flow

Educators are not performers.
They are **instructional leaders**.

Teach Like Ced™ asks educators to:
- Trust the structure
- Teach with intention
- Resist the urge to rush

When the flow is honored, growth follows.

Conclusion: Rhythm Creates Results

Literacy instruction improves when:
- Students know the process
- Teachers know the purpose
- Learning has momentum

The Monday–Friday instructional flow is the engine that powers Teach Like Ced™.

The next chapter will move deeper into **classroom execution**, beginning with how to use the **Teacher's Edition** to maintain fidelity while honoring professional expertise.

SECTION III

CLASSROOM PRACTICE

Structure lives in execution.

> This section translates philosophy and model into daily classroom practice. It clarifies how educators use the Teacher's Edition with fidelity, leverage the Student Workbook as a cognitive workspace, and manage time intentionally to protect literacy instruction.

CHAPTER 7

Using the Teacher's Edition with Fidelity and Professional Autonomy

Teach Like Ced™ Educator Handbook

Cedric A. Washington
Who Lives Like This?! Publishing LLC

Introduction: Fidelity Is Not the Enemy of Professionalism

One of the most sensitive conversations in education centers on fidelity.

Teachers are rightfully wary of programs that:
- Script every word
- Reduce educators to technicians
- Strip classrooms of humanity

Teach Like Ced™ does not ask teachers to surrender their expertise.
It asks them to **anchor it**.

This chapter establishes a critical distinction:

Fidelity protects students. Professional autonomy empowers teachers. Teach Like Ced™ requires both.

The Teacher's Edition exists to ensure instructional clarity, equity, and consistency—while still honoring the educator's role as a thinking professional.

Why the Teacher's Edition Exists

The Teacher's Edition (TE) was not created because teachers lack skill.

It was created because:
- Not all teachers were trained equally
- Not all classrooms receive the same instructional support
- Not all students can afford instructional inconsistency

The TE serves as:
- A guardrail against dilution
- A support for novice teachers
- A consistency tool for systems

Teach Like Ced™ recognizes that **great instruction should not depend on chance**.

What Fidelity Actually Means in Teach Like Ced™

Fidelity in Teach Like Ced™ does not mean reading from a script word-for-word.

Fidelity means:
- Honoring the instructional sequence
- Teaching the skills in the intended order
- Maintaining structure while adapting delivery

Teachers may personalize:
- Tone
- Examples
- Pacing adjustments

Teachers may not remove:
- Sentence work
- Oral rehearsal
- Revision
- Structure

Fidelity ensures the framework works as designed.

The Teacher's Edition as an Instructional Coach

The TE functions as a **silent instructional coach**.

It provides:
- Model language for teaching concepts
- Anticipated student responses
- Common misconceptions
- Suggested pacing

Teachers are encouraged to:
- Study the TE
- Understand the "why" behind each step
- Use it as preparation, not dependency

Over time, teachers internalize the framework and deliver it naturally.

Modeling: Showing Thinking, Not Just Assigning Work

One of the most critical components of the TE is modeling.

Teach Like Ced™ insists that teachers:
- Write in front of students
- Think aloud
- Make mistakes publicly

The TE provides sample modeling language so teachers can:
- See how to verbalize thinking
- Normalize confusion
- Demonstrate revision

Modeling demystifies writing and builds trust.

Anticipating Misconceptions to Prevent Frustration

Many instructional breakdowns occur because teachers are forced to react instead of prepare.

The TE anticipates:
- Likely student errors
- Conceptual misunderstandings
- Language confusion

This allows teachers to:
- Intervene early
- Clarify immediately
- Maintain momentum

Preventative clarity is more effective than reactive correction.

Balancing Structure and Teacher Voice

Teach Like Ced™ respects teacher voice.

Educators are encouraged to:
- Use culturally relevant examples
- Connect lessons to current contexts
- Adapt explanations to student needs

However, personalization must not replace:
- Explicit instruction
- Structured writing
- Clear modeling

Teacher voice enhances the framework—it does not rewrite it.

Common Misuses of the Teacher's Edition

To maintain integrity, Teach Like Ced™ identifies common errors:
- Skipping TE guidance because "students already know this"
- Improvising before understanding the structure
- Using the workbook without TE alignment

- Treating the TE as optional

These practices undermine outcomes.

Structure must be learned before it can be adapted.

Supporting New and Veteran Teachers Alike

The TE supports:
- New teachers by providing clarity and confidence
- Veteran teachers by refining practice and pacing

Teach Like Ced™ does not assume experience equals mastery.

Even skilled educators benefit from:
- Shared language
- Common structure
- Collective fidelity

This builds instructional coherence across schools and districts.

The Equity Case for Fidelity

Fidelity is an equity issue.

When instruction varies wildly:
- Some students receive rigorous literacy instruction
- Others receive fragmented experiences

Teach Like Ced™ ensures that:
- Every student has access to the same core instructional quality
- Literacy is not dependent on classroom assignment

Consistency is not conformity, it is **justice**.

The Educator's Responsibility

Teach Like Ced™ asks educators to:
- Respect the framework
- Commit to the process
- Trust the structure

Autonomy is not the freedom to abandon best practice.
It is the freedom to **execute it well**.

Conclusion: Fidelity Sustains Impact

The Teacher's Edition exists to protect the work.

When used with intention, it:
- Strengthens instruction
- Reduces burnout
- Elevates outcomes

Teach Like Ced™ succeeds when educators lead with both **discipline and discernment**.

The next chapter turns attention to the **Student Workbook**, where daily practice becomes visible growth.

CHAPTER 8

Using the Student Workbook as a Cognitive Workspace

Teach Like Ced™ Educator Handbook

Cedric A. Washington
Who Lives Like This?! Publishing LLC

Introduction: The Difference Between Workbooks and Thinking Tools

In many classrooms, workbooks are treated as compliance tools.

Pages are assigned.
Answers are written.
Books are collected.

Completion becomes the goal, and thinking becomes incidental.

Teach Like Ced™ rejects this approach.

The Student Workbook is not busywork.
It is not homework filler.
It is not a silent packet.

It is a **cognitive workspace**—a place where thinking is rehearsed, refined, revised, and recorded over time.

This chapter clarifies how the Student Workbook functions within the Teach Like Ced™ framework and why its intentional use is essential to literacy growth.

Why Students Need a Dedicated Thinking Space

Students think best when they have a place to:
- Try ideas without fear
- Make mistakes safely
- See growth over time
- Revisit previous thinking

The Student Workbook provides this space.

Unlike loose-leaf papers or digital submissions that disappear, the workbook becomes:
- A literacy archive
- A progress tracker
- A confidence builder

Students do not just complete work—they **build evidence of mastery**.

The Workbook as a Daily Literacy Practice Tool

Teach Like Ced™ requires daily writing.

Not daily essays.
Not daily tests.
Daily **intentional writing**.

The workbook supports this by:
- Structuring daily sentence practice
- Guiding paragraph development
- Prompting reflection and revision

Writing becomes routine, not intimidating.

How Structure in the Workbook Supports Equity

The Student Workbook is intentionally structured to:
- Reduce ambiguity
- Clarify expectations
- Support all learners

Clear prompts and consistent layouts help students:
- Focus on thinking instead of guessing
- Understand what quality looks like
- Engage independently

Structure is not limiting—it is **liberating**, especially for students who have been historically underserved.

Sentence Work: Where Confidence Is Built

Every workbook lesson begins with sentence-level work.

This is intentional.

Sentence practice:
- Builds clarity
- Reinforces structure
- Strengthens comprehension

Students learn that strong writing starts small.

Teachers should expect:

- Imperfect sentences
- Gradual improvement
- Increasing confidence

The workbook captures this progression visibly.

Paragraph Development in the Workbook

As students advance, the workbook guides them to:
- Expand ideas
- Develop paragraphs
- Connect sentences logically

Paragraph work is scaffolded so students:
- Are not overwhelmed
- Can see how ideas grow
- Learn to stay focused

Students begin to understand that writing is not about length, it is about **development**.

Reflection as a Core Component

Teach Like Ced™ embeds reflection intentionally.

Reflection is not an add-on.
It is instruction.

Workbook reflection prompts ask students to:
- Evaluate their thinking
- Identify growth
- Set goals

This builds metacognition—students begin to understand **how they learn**, not just what they learn.

Revision: Teaching Students That Writing Is a Process

The workbook is designed for revision.

Students are encouraged to:
- Reread their work
- Clarify ideas
- Improve expression

Teachers should not treat first drafts as final products.

Revision teaches:
- SELF Governing
- Persistence
- Ownership

Students learn that improvement is expected.

Using the Workbook for Differentiation

The workbook supports differentiation naturally.

Teachers may:
- Assign fewer sentences
- Extend paragraph work
- Add challenge prompts

However, the structure remains intact.

Differentiation adjusts the **depth**, not the foundation.

Common Misuses of the Student Workbook

To protect fidelity, Teach Like Ced™ identifies common errors:
- Assigning pages without instruction
- Using the workbook as independent seatwork only
- Grading for completion instead of clarity
- Skipping reflection sections

These practices undermine the purpose of the workbook.

The Teacher's Role During Workbook Use

When students are working in the workbook, teachers should:
- Circulate
- Confer
- Ask probing questions
- Offer targeted feedback

This is not a quiet time to disengage.

The workbook is most powerful when paired with **active teaching**.

The Workbook as Evidence of Growth

Over time, the Student Workbook becomes:
- A record of progress
- A portfolio of thinking
- A source of pride

Students can look back and see:
- Where they started
- How they improved
- What they are capable of

This visibility builds belief.

Conclusion: From Pages to Power

The Student Workbook transforms writing from an assignment into a **practice**.

It teaches students that:
- Their thoughts matter
- Growth is possible
- Clarity is achievable

When used with fidelity, the workbook becomes a daily act of empowerment.

The next chapter will address how to manage time effectively within the literacy block—ensuring that Teach Like Ced™ thrives within real classroom constraints.

CHAPTER 9

Time Management in the Literacy Block

Teach Like Ced™ Educator Handbook

Cedric A. Washington
Who Lives Like This?! Publishing LLC

Introduction: Time Is Not the Problem—Clarity Is

Educators often say:
- "There isn't enough time."
- "We're always behind."
- "We have too much to cover."

While these frustrations are real, Teach Like Ced™ challenges the underlying assumption that **time itself is the issue**.

In most classrooms, time is lost not to lack of minutes, but to:
- Unclear instructional priorities
- Overloaded lessons
- Constant transitions
- Activities without purpose

Teach Like Ced™ does not ask educators to do more.
It asks them to **do what matters most—well**.

Why Literacy Time Must Be Protected

Literacy is not one subject among many.
It is the foundation through which all learning occurs.

When literacy time is fragmented:
- Writing becomes rushed
- Thinking becomes shallow
- Students disengage

Teach Like Ced™ treats the literacy block as **sacred instructional space**—not easily surrendered to interruptions or filler activities.

Protecting literacy time is an equity issue.
Students who need it most often lose it first.

The Teach Like Ced™ Principle of Focused Instruction

Teach Like Ced™ operates on a principle of focus:

Every minute must serve thinking, writing, or language development.

This means eliminating:
- Excessive worksheets
- Redundant activities
- Long lectures without engagement

Instead, time is spent on:
- Modeling
- Guided practice
- Writing
- Revision
- Reflection

Focused instruction produces deeper learning in less time.

Anatomy of an Effective Literacy Block

Teach Like Ced™ adapts to different schedules, but the structure remains consistent.

Sample 60-Minute Literacy Block:
- **10 minutes** – Oral language, review, and activation
- **15 minutes** – Explicit modeling and instruction
- **20 minutes** – Guided and independent writing
- **10 minutes** – Feedback, conferencing, or revision
- **5 minutes** – Reflection or closure

This balance ensures that:
- Students are actively engaged
- Writing is prioritized
- Reflection reinforces learning

Adapting the Framework to Shorter Blocks

Teach Like Ced™ is flexible by design.

In a **45-minute block**:
- Combine modeling and oral rehearsal
- Shorten independent writing slightly
- Maintain reflection

In a **30-minute intervention or tutoring session**:
- Focus on one sentence or one paragraph
- Prioritize clarity over quantity

- Keep the structure intact

The key is not length, it is **intentionality**.

Transitions: Where Time Is Won or Lost

Poor transitions drain instructional time.

Teach Like Ced™ emphasizes:
- Clear routines
- Predictable flow
- Minimal downtime

When students know:
- What comes next
- Where materials are
- What is expected

Transitions become seamless.

Time is reclaimed without stress.

Avoiding the Trap of Overplanning

More activities do not equal better instruction.

Teach Like Ced™ warns against:
- Overpacked lessons
- Multiple objectives in one block
- Teaching breadth at the expense of depth

One well-taught sentence is more valuable than:
- Three rushed activities
- Ten unanswered questions
- An unfinished worksheet

Depth produces retention.

The Role of Consistency in Time Management

Consistency saves time.

When routines are stable:
- Students settle faster
- Instructions are understood

- Less time is spent redirecting behavior

Teach Like Ced™ uses repetition intentionally—not as monotony, but as **efficiency**.

Balancing Rigor and Stamina

Teach Like Ced™ respects student stamina.

Long stretches of passive listening are avoided.

Instead:
- Instruction alternates between input and output
- Writing is broken into manageable chunks
- Oral language reenergizes engagement

This balance prevents burnout and sustains focus.

Common Time Management Mistakes

Teach Like Ced™ identifies frequent errors:
- Spending too long on directions
- Correcting every mistake publicly
- Rushing through writing to "finish"

These practices consume time without producing growth.

Clarity, not speed, is the goal.

The Educator's Role in Managing Time

Educators are time architects.

Teach Like Ced™ asks teachers to:
- Plan with purpose
- Execute with discipline
- Reflect on what truly moves learning forward

Time management is not about control—it is about **intentional leadership**.

Conclusion: Time Used Well Multiplies Impact

When literacy time is:
- Focused

- Structured
- Protected

Students grow faster than expected.

Teach Like Ced™ proves that effective literacy instruction does not require more hours—only **better use of the ones we have**.

The next chapter will address how Teach Like Ced™ supports **differentiation and intervention** without sacrificing rigor or identity.

SECTION IV

ASSESSMENT & STUDENT GROWTH

Assessment should illuminate thinking, not punish struggle.

> This section reframes differentiation, intervention, assessment, and oral presentation as tools for growth. It shows how Teach Like Ced™ maintains rigor while honoring student dignity, voice, and intellectual confidence.

CHAPTER 10

Differentiation and Intervention Without Lowering the Ceiling

Teach Like Ced™ Educator Handbook

Cedric A. Washington
Who Lives Like This?! Publishing LLC

Introduction: The Myth That Holds Students Back

In too many classrooms, differentiation has become a euphemism for **less**.

Less writing.
Less thinking.
Less expectation.

This is often justified as support, yet its long-term effect is the opposite: it **cements inequity**.

Teach Like Ced™ rejects the idea that students need less rigor to succeed. Instead, it asserts a fundamental principle:

> **Students need clearer structure—not lower ceilings.**
>
> This chapter explains how Teach Like Ced™ differentiates instruction and delivers intervention while maintaining intellectual integrity, cultural respect, and high expectations for all learners.

Why Traditional Differentiation Often Fails

Traditional differentiation models frequently rely on:
- Different assignments for different students
- Reduced expectations for struggling learners
- Enrichment activities disconnected from core instruction

While well-intentioned, these practices often:
- Isolate students
- Dilute instruction
- Create invisible tracking within classrooms

Teach Like Ced™ identifies the flaw:
Differentiation is applied to outcomes instead of access.

The Teach Like Ced™ Differentiation Principle

Teach Like Ced™ differentiates by adjusting:
- **Support**
- **Scaffolding**
- **Pacing**

—not the intellectual demand.

All students engage with:
- The same core skills
- The same instructional framework
- The same literacy goals

What changes is **how** students get there.

Structure as the Primary Differentiator

Structure is the most equitable form of differentiation.

Clear structure:
- Reduces confusion
- Supports independence
- Prevents overwhelm

Teach Like Ced™ uses:
- Sentence frames
- Modeled examples
- Step-by-step progression

These tools support struggling students without signaling deficiency.

Sentence-Level Intervention: Where Growth Accelerates

Teach Like Ced™ intervenes at the sentence level first.

Why?

Because:
- Sentences reveal thinking gaps
- Sentence mastery builds confidence
- Sentence work is manageable and measurable

Struggling writers are not pushed into longer tasks prematurely.
They are guided to **clarity one sentence at a time**.

This approach prevents frustration and accelerates growth.

Oral Language as an Intervention Tool

Many students struggle with writing not because they lack ideas, but because they struggle to translate thought into text.

Teach Like Ced™ uses oral language strategically by:
- Allowing students to speak ideas before writing
- Coaching academic language in real time
- Rehearsing sentences aloud

This honors cultural strengths and builds confidence without lowering standards.

Scaffolding Without Dependency

Scaffolds are temporary.

Teach Like Ced™ ensures that supports:
- Are gradually removed
- Promote independence
- Do not become permanent crutches

Teachers monitor when students are ready to:
- Write without frames
- Develop ideas independently
- Take greater ownership

The goal is **autonomy**, not reliance.

Supporting Advanced Learners Without Detachment

Advanced learners are often given:
- Extra work
- Unrelated enrichment
- Independent projects

Teach Like Ced™ instead deepens:
- Sentence complexity
- Analytical demands
- Precision of language

Advanced students remain connected to the core framework while extending their thinking.

Intervention as Instruction, Not Remediation

Teach Like Ced™ reframes intervention.

Intervention is not:
- Pulling students away from real instruction
- Isolating skills in worksheets
- Reducing expectations

Intervention is:
- Clearer instruction
- Slower pacing
- More modeling
- More feedback

This keeps students within the learning community while receiving targeted support.

The Role of the Teacher in Differentiated Instruction

Educators are not asked to create multiple lesson plans.

They are asked to:
- Know their students
- Use structure intentionally
- Adjust supports thoughtfully

Teach Like Ced™ simplifies differentiation so teachers can focus on **teaching**, not managing complexity.

Protecting Student Dignity

Differentiation must never signal deficiency.

Teach Like Ced™ ensures that:
- All students engage with meaningful work
- Support is normalized
- Growth is celebrated publicly

Students do not feel singled out, they feel **supported**.

What Differentiation Without Lowering the Ceiling Looks Like

In Teach Like Ced™ classrooms:
- All students write daily
- All students engage with structure
- All students are expected to grow

Support is invisible.
Expectations are visible.

Conclusion: Rigor With Humanity

True differentiation does not ask:

"How little can this student do?"

It asks:

"What does this student need to reach the same intellectual destination?"

Teach Like Ced™ proves that when structure replaces assumption, and clarity replaces reduction, **all students rise**.

The next chapter will turn to **assessment**, showing how growth is measured without punishment and accountability is humanized through writing, speaking, and reflection.

CHAPTER 11

Assessment for Growth, Not Punishment

Teach Like Ced™ Educator Handbook

Cedric A. Washington
Who Lives Like This?! Publishing LLC

Introduction: What Assessment Was Never Meant to Be

Assessment was never intended to be a weapon.

Yet for many students, assessment has become synonymous with:
- Anxiety
- Judgment
- Labels
- Permanent conclusions

Teach Like Ced™ challenges this misuse.

Assessment, when designed and used properly, is a **mirror**—not a verdict. It reflects where thinking is clear, where it is developing, and where instruction must respond.

This chapter establishes a guiding principle:

Assessment should inform instruction and empower students—not punish them for where they are.

The Problem with Traditional Assessment Models

Traditional assessment systems often emphasize:
- Speed over depth
- Correctness over reasoning
- Scores over growth

These systems reward test-taking proficiency more than genuine understanding and often obscure the most important question in literacy instruction:

Can the student explain what they think and why?

Teach Like Ced™ identifies a fundamental flaw:
Many assessments measure **compliance**, not **comprehension**.

Writing as the Most Honest Form of Assessment

Teach Like Ced™ centers writing as the primary assessment tool because writing makes thinking visible.

A written response reveals:
- What the student understands
- How ideas are connected
- Where reasoning breaks down
- How language is being used

Unlike selected-response tests, writing does not allow students to hide behind chance or strategy.

Writing is not hard, it is **clearer**.

Formative Assessment: Catching Misunderstanding Early

Teach Like Ced™ prioritizes formative assessment—assessment used *during* learning.

Examples include:
- One-sentence responses
- Short paragraph explanations
- Oral explanations paired with writing

These checks allow teachers to:
- Adjust instruction immediately
- Clarify misconceptions
- Prevent gaps from widening

Formative assessment is not about grading.
It is about **guidance**.

Weekly Checks: Measuring Progress Without Pressure

Weekly assessments in Teach Like Ced™ are:
- Short
- Focused
- Aligned to instruction

Students may be asked to:
- Write one clear sentence
- Expand a paragraph
- Explain reasoning orally

The goal is not perfection—it is **progress**.

Students learn that assessment is part of learning, not an interruption of it.

Unit Assessments: Demonstrating Thinking Over Time

Teach Like Ced™ unit assessments ask students to demonstrate:
- Idea development
- Writing clarity
- Use of structure
- Growth in voice

Rather than one high-stakes moment, unit assessments represent a **culmination of practice**.

Students are prepared because the assessment mirrors daily work.

Rubrics That Value Thinking

Teach Like Ced™ rubrics emphasize:
- Clarity of ideas
- Organization
- Use of evidence
- Growth over time

Mechanical errors are addressed—but they do not overshadow meaning.

This communicates an important message to students:

Your thinking matters.

Oral Assessment as Intellectual Evidence

Teach Like Ced™ treats speaking as a legitimate form of assessment.

Students are asked to:
- Explain their writing
- Defend their ideas
- Respond to questions

Oral assessment:
- Reduces anxiety for some learners
- Reveals understanding that writing may mask
- Builds confidence and ownership

Speaking and writing work together to show comprehension.

Student Reflection as Self-Assessment

Teach Like Ced™ teaches students to assess themselves.

Reflection prompts ask students to consider:
- What they improved
- What challenged them
- What strategy helped

This builds metacognition—students begin to understand how they learn.

Self-assessment shifts students from passive recipients to **active participants** in growth.

Feedback That Fuels Growth

Teach Like Ced™ emphasizes feedback that is:
- Specific
- Timely
- Actionable

Feedback focuses on:
- One or two key areas
- Clarity before correctness
- Next steps, not mistakes

Students are not overwhelmed.
They are guided.

Grades as Communication, Not Identity

Teach Like Ced™ recognizes that grades are often required.

However, grades must be framed as:
- Information
- Feedback
- A snapshot in time

Grades do not define students.
They describe progress.

This distinction protects student identity and motivation.

The Equity Dimension of Assessment

Assessment practices disproportionately harm students when:
- Language is valued over reasoning
- Speed is prioritized over clarity
- Growth is ignored

Teach Like Ced™ designs assessment to:
- Reveal understanding
- Support instruction
- Honor diverse learners

Equity is built through **clarity**, not accommodation alone.

The Educator's Role in Humanizing Assessment

Educators are not judges.
They are **interpreters of learning**.

Teach Like Ced™ asks teachers to:
- Use assessment as insight
- Respond instructionally
- Communicate growth clearly

Assessment becomes part of teaching—not a separate event.

Conclusion: Assessment as Empowerment

When assessment is aligned with instruction, students:
- Understand expectations
- See their growth
- Trust the learning process

Teach Like Ced™ restores assessment to its rightful place—as a tool for empowerment, not fear.

The next chapter will focus on **oral presentations and student voice**, demonstrating how speaking reinforces literacy, confidence, and ownership.

CHAPTER 12

Oral Presentation, Student Voice, and Intellectual Confidence

Teach Like Ced™ Educator Handbook

Cedric A. Washington
Who Lives Like This?! Publishing LLC

Introduction: If Students Can't Explain It, They Don't Own It

One of the most revealing moments in any classroom is when a student is asked to explain their thinking aloud.

Not read it.
Not select it.
Explain it.

This moment exposes the truth:
students may complete work without fully owning understanding.

Teach Like Ced™ treats oral presentation as **intellectual evidence**—proof that students can organize thought, select language intentionally, and communicate meaning with confidence.

This chapter establishes a core principle:

> **Voice is not optional in literacy. It is foundational.**

Why Speaking Strengthens Reading and Writing

Speaking, reading, and writing are not separate skills.
They are interdependent literacy practices.

When students speak about what they read or wrote, they must:
- Organize ideas coherently
- Use precise vocabulary
- Monitor clarity in real time
- Respond to questions thoughtfully

This cognitive work strengthens comprehension and sharpens writing.

Teach Like Ced™ uses speaking as a **rehearsal space** for thinking—where ideas are tested before they are finalized on paper.

Oral Language as the Bridge to Confidence

Many students struggle with writing not because they lack ideas, but because they lack confidence in expressing them.

Speaking provides a lower barrier of entry.

Teach Like Ced™ leverages oral language to:
- Reduce fear of mistakes
- Normalize imperfect thinking
- Build momentum toward written expression

Students gain confidence when they realize:

"I already know how to explain this—I just need help writing it."

Student Voice vs. Noise

Teach Like Ced™ makes an important distinction.

Student voice is not:
- Talking without purpose
- Sharing without structure
- Opinion without reasoning

Student voice is:
- Organized
- Purposeful
- Grounded in evidence

Oral presentation is structured, intentional, and aligned to learning goals.

This ensures that speaking builds literacy rather than disrupting it.

Teaching Students How to Speak Academically

Teach Like Ced™ teaches oral language explicitly.

Students learn how to:
- Begin explanations clearly
- Support ideas with reasons
- Clarify when misunderstood
- Respond respectfully to questions

Example Sentence Stems:
- *I believe ___ because ___.*
- *The evidence shows ___.*
- *I agree/disagree because ___.*

These stems provide structure without scripting.

Oral Presentation as a Daily Practice

Teach Like Ced™ does not reserve speaking for special occasions.

Oral language is embedded daily through:
- Turn-and-talks
- Think-pair-share
- Small-group discussions
- Brief individual explanations

These low-stakes opportunities prepare students for more formal presentations.

Formal Oral Presentations: Purpose and Design

Formal presentations in Teach Like Ced™ are:
- Short
- Structured
- Aligned to writing tasks

Students may present:
- A paragraph explanation
- A revised sentence
- A position statement

The goal is not performance, it is **clarity**.

Reducing Presentation Anxiety

Teach Like Ced™ acknowledges that public speaking can be intimidating.

Teachers support students by:
- Modeling presentations
- Allowing rehearsal
- Creating respectful norms
- Emphasizing growth over perfection

Confidence is built through **consistency**, not pressure.

Assessing Oral Presentation Fairly

Teach Like Ced™ assesses oral presentations using clear criteria such as:
- Clarity of ideas
- Organization
- Use of evidence
- Engagement with audience

Assessment focuses on communication—not personality.

This ensures students are evaluated on what matters.

Oral Presentation and SELF Mastery

Oral presentation reinforces all five SELF pillars:
- **SELF Conscience:** Owning ideas
- **SELF Governing:** Managing nerves and responses
- **Social Conscience:** Considering audience
- **Aspirations:** Speaking with purpose
- **Good People Skills:** Listening and responding respectfully

Speaking becomes an act of empowerment.

Cultural Strengths in Oral Expression

Many students come from cultures where:
- Oral storytelling is valued
- Verbal explanation is strong
- Dialogue is natural

Teach Like Ced™ honors these strengths by:
- Using oral language as a literacy asset
- Teaching how to refine speech academically
- Validating voice while elevating clarity

Students are not silent, they are **trained**.

The Educator's Role in Cultivating Voice

Educators are responsible for:
- Creating safe speaking environments
- Teaching speaking skills explicitly
- Modeling respectful listening

Teach Like Ced™ classrooms are places where:
- Ideas are heard
- Questions are welcomed

- Thinking is visible

Conclusion: Voice Is Proof of Ownership

When students can speak clearly about what they think, they demonstrate ownership of learning.

Teach Like Ced™ ensures that literacy instruction produces students who:
- Write with purpose
- Read with intention
- Speak with confidence

The next chapter will address **fidelity and impact**, clarifying what Teach Like Ced™ is—and is not—so the framework remains intact as it scales.

SECTION V

FIDELITY & IMPACT

What is protected, endures.

This section safeguards the framework. It defines what Teach Like Ced™ is—and is not—while establishing fidelity as an equity commitment and outlining how the work sustains long-term impact without dilution.

CHAPTER 13

Fidelity, Integrity, and Long-Term Impact

Teach Like Ced™ Educator Handbook

Cedric A. Washington
Who Lives Like This?! Publishing LLC

Introduction: Why Good Frameworks Fail Without Integrity

Many educational frameworks begin with promise.

They are well-designed.
They are research-aligned.
They produce early success.

Then they fail—not because they were flawed, but because they were **watered down**.

Teach Like Ced™ was built with this reality in mind.

This chapter establishes a non-negotiable truth:

> **Impact is not sustained by popularity. It is sustained by fidelity.**
>
> Without integrity in implementation, even the strongest pedagogy collapses into inconsistency.

What Fidelity Means in Teach Like Ced™

Fidelity does not mean rigidity.

It means honoring the **core design** of the framework.

Teach Like Ced™ fidelity requires:
- Maintaining the Sentence → Paragraph → Essay progression
- Preserving the Monday–Friday instructional rhythm
- Centering writing as the primary literacy driver
- Integrating SELF into daily instruction
- Treating culture as pedagogy, not decoration

Fidelity ensures that the framework functions as intended.

What Fidelity Does Not Mean

To avoid confusion, Teach Like Ced™ is explicit.

Fidelity does not mean:
- Teaching word-for-word scripts
- Removing teacher creativity
- Ignoring student context
- Treating the framework as inflexible

Fidelity means:
- Respecting structure
- Understanding purpose
- Adapting delivery without dismantling design

This balance protects both **students and educators**.

Why Partial Implementation Produces Partial Results

One of the most common threats to instructional impact is selective implementation.

Examples include:
- Using sentence frames but skipping oral rehearsal
- Assigning workbook pages without modeling
- Teaching writing without revision
- Using culture as examples but removing structure

These practices fragment the framework.

Teach Like Ced™ is a **system**, not a menu.

When pieces are removed, results suffer—and the framework is blamed instead of the misuse.

Integrity as an Equity Issue

Instructional inconsistency disproportionately harms students who:
- Need structure the most
- Have limited academic language exposure
- Depend on school for access to rigorous instruction

Teach Like Ced™ treats integrity as an equity commitment.

Every student deserves:
- Clear instruction
- Consistent expectations
- Access to the full framework

Equity cannot exist without fidelity.

Protecting Teach Like Ced™ from Mischaracterization

As Teach Like Ced™ expands, it may be labeled inaccurately.

This chapter establishes what Teach Like Ced™ is **not**:
- Not a political agenda
- Not a compliance-based SEL program
- Not a writing-only initiative
- Not culturally performative instruction

Teach Like Ced™ is:
- Literacy-first
- Structure-driven
- Culturally intelligent
- Research-aligned
- Human-centered

Clear definition prevents distortion.

The Role of Leadership in Sustaining Fidelity

Long-term impact requires leadership alignment.

School and district leaders must:
- Protect literacy time
- Support professional development
- Avoid initiative overload
- Reinforce instructional consistency

Teach Like Ced™ thrives when leaders understand that:

Frameworks fail when systems fragment them.

Leadership clarity sustains classroom success.

Professional Development as a Fidelity Tool

Teach Like Ced™ professional development is not optional training.

It is the mechanism through which:
- Shared language is built
- Expectations are clarified
- Practice is refined

Ongoing PD ensures that the framework evolves **without losing its core**.

Measuring Impact Beyond Test Scores

Teach Like Ced™ impact is visible in:
- Student writing clarity
- Oral confidence
- Ownership of thinking
- Reduction in avoidance behaviors
- Increased engagement

While assessment data matters, these indicators reveal **true literacy growth**.

Sustainability Through Culture, Not Compliance

Teach Like Ced™ sustains because it:
- Honors student identity
- Respects teacher professionalism
- Provides structure without control

Frameworks endure when they become part of school culture—not enforced mandates.

The Long View: Teaching for Legacy, Not Trends

Teach Like Ced™ was not designed for short-term adoption cycles.

It was designed to:
- Train generations of educators
- Empower generations of students
- Restore integrity to literacy instruction

This work is about **legacy**, not novelty.

The Educator's Commitment

Teach Like Ced™ asks educators to commit to:
- Teaching with intention
- Upholding structure
- Honoring voice
- Protecting integrity

When educators commit fully, students rise consistently

Conclusion: Integrity Is the Impact

Teach Like Ced™ will not succeed because it is popular.

It will succeed because:
- It is sound
- It is intentional
- It is complete

Integrity is what ensures that literacy instruction remains **liberating**, not limiting.

This chapter secures the work.

APPENDIX A

Research Alignment and Academic Foundations

Teach Like Ced™ Educator Handbook

Cedric A. Washington
Who Lives Like This?! Publishing LLC

Purpose of This Appendix

Teach Like Ced™ is not built on ideology, trend, or intuition alone.
It is grounded in decades of interdisciplinary research across:
- Literacy development
- Cognitive science
- Writing-to-learn theory
- Oral language acquisition
- Culturally responsive pedagogy
- Motivation and identity research

This appendix clarifies **how** Teach Like Ced™ aligns with established research—and more importantly—**how it translates research into daily instructional practice**.

1. Science of Reading Alignment

The Science of Reading emphasizes that proficient literacy requires explicit, systematic instruction in:
- Phonological awareness
- Phonics
- Fluency
- Vocabulary
- Comprehension

Teach Like Ced™ fully affirms these components and extends them into **meaning-making and expression**.

Alignment in Practice:
- **Vocabulary** is reinforced through daily writing, not isolated memorization
- **Comprehension** is demonstrated through sentence and paragraph construction
- **Fluency** improves as students repeatedly read, speak, and write language with purpose

Teach Like Ced™ does not replace foundational reading instruction.
It **activates it** by ensuring students can articulate understanding, not just decode text.

2. Writing-to-Learn Research

Writing-to-learn research establishes that writing is not only a communication skill but a **cognitive process** that deepens understanding.

Key findings include:
- Writing clarifies thinking
- Writing reveals misconceptions
- Writing improves retention

Teach Like Ced™ operationalizes this research by:
- Making writing daily and structured
- Using sentence-level writing as formative assessment
- Treating writing as evidence of comprehension

Students are not writing *after* learning.
They are writing **to learn**.

3. Cognitive Load Theory

Cognitive Load Theory explains that learning is impeded when working memory is overwhelmed.

Teach Like Ced™ reduces cognitive overload by:
- Teaching one skill at a time
- Using predictable instructional routines
- Scaffolding complexity gradually

The Sentence → Paragraph → Essay framework aligns directly with cognitive load principles by:
- Chunking learning
- Sequencing complexity
- Preventing premature demands

This allows students to focus on **thinking**, not confusion.

4. Oral Language Development Research

Research consistently shows that oral language proficiency is a strong predictor of reading comprehension and writing ability.

Teach Like Ced™ integrates oral language as:
- A rehearsal space for ideas
- A bridge between thought and text
- A culturally responsive literacy practice

Oral rehearsal:
- Strengthens syntax
- Clarifies reasoning
- Builds confidence

Speaking is not treated as a precursor to "real work."
It is treated as **real literacy work**.

5. Metacognition and Self-Regulated Learning

Metacognitive research emphasizes that students learn more effectively when they understand:
- How they learn
- Why strategies work
- When to adjust approaches

Teach Like Ced™ embeds metacognition through:
- Student reflection prompts
- Revision practices
- SELF Governing instruction

Students are taught to monitor their thinking, not just complete tasks.

6. Motivation, Identity, and Agency Research

Research in educational psychology confirms that students are more motivated when they:
- Feel competent
- Feel autonomous
- See relevance in learning

Teach Like Ced™ addresses motivation by:
- Building confidence through structure
- Encouraging ownership of ideas
- Connecting literacy to identity and aspiration

The SELF framework ensures that literacy instruction develops **agency**, not dependency.

7. Culturally Responsive Pedagogy

Culturally responsive research emphasizes:
- Leveraging students' cultural assets
- Valuing diverse communication styles
- Teaching academic language explicitly

Teach Like Ced™ aligns by:

- Using culture as an instructional entry point
- Honoring oral traditions
- Teaching academic language as an addition, not a replacement

This approach accelerates learning while preserving student identity.

8. Formative Assessment Research

Formative assessment research highlights the importance of:
- Frequent checks for understanding
- Feedback that guides learning
- Student involvement in assessment

Teach Like Ced™ centers formative assessment through:
- Daily writing
- Oral explanations
- Reflection

Assessment informs instruction continuously—not just at the end of a unit.

9. Gradual Release of Responsibility

Teach Like Ced™ aligns with Gradual Release models by:
- Modeling explicitly
- Guiding practice intentionally
- Supporting independence responsibly

However, Teach Like Ced™ emphasizes that **release must be earned**, not rushed.

Structure is maintained until mastery emerges.

10. Equity-Focused Instructional Design

Equity research confirms that:
- Clear expectations improve outcomes
- Structure benefits all learners
- Access precedes achievement

Teach Like Ced™ operationalizes equity by:
- Teaching structure explicitly
- Normalizing support
- Maintaining high expectations for all students

Equity is achieved through **clarity and consistency**, not lowered standards.

Conclusion: Research Applied, Not Just Referenced

Teach Like Ced™ is research-aligned not because it cites studies—but because it **implements their findings with precision**.

This framework demonstrates that:
- Literacy grows through structure
- Understanding is revealed through writing
- Confidence is built through voice
- Culture is an asset in learning

Appendix A establishes Teach Like Ced™ as a **defensible, credible, and scalable literacy framework** grounded in both scholarship and classroom reality.

APPENDIX B

Standards Crosswalk: Reading, Writing, Speaking & Listening

Teach Like Ced™ Educator Handbook

Cedric A. Washington
Who Lives Like This?! Publishing LLC

Purpose of This Crosswalk

Teach Like Ced™ was not created in opposition to standards.
It was created in response to **how standards are often misapplied**.

This appendix shows how Teach Like Ced™:
- Meets grade-level literacy standards
- Clarifies expectations for educators
- Strengthens student outcomes beyond compliance

Rather than listing standards in isolation, Teach Like Ced™ **operationalizes them** through daily instructional practice.

1. Writing Standards Alignment

Core Writing Expectations (Across Grades)

Students are expected to:
- Write clear arguments and explanations
- Support ideas with reasons and evidence
- Organize writing logically
- Revise and edit for clarity

Teach Like Ced™ Alignment

Sentence → Paragraph → Essay Framework
- Teaches idea development incrementally
- Ensures students understand structure before complexity
- Aligns directly to opinion, informative, and argumentative writing standards

Daily Writing Practice
- Meets expectations for routine writing
- Builds stamina and fluency
- Normalizes revision as part of the writing process

Explicit Modeling
- Supports standards requiring students to "develop and strengthen writing"

- Makes expectations visible and attainable

Result: Writing standards are not rushed—they are mastered.

2. Reading Standards Alignment

Core Reading Expectations

Students are expected to:
- Determine central ideas
- Analyze text structure
- Cite evidence
- Interpret author's purpose

Teach Like Ced™ Alignment

Writing as Evidence of Reading
- Students demonstrate comprehension through written explanation
- Reading is assessed through reasoning, not recall

Sentence-Level Comprehension Checks
- Reveal understanding immediately
- Prevent misconceptions from compounding

Oral + Written Responses
- Strengthen interpretation
- Encourage deeper engagement with text

Result: Reading standards are achieved through **active meaning-making**, not passive consumption.

3. Speaking & Listening Standards Alignment

Core Speaking & Listening Expectations

Students are expected to:
- Engage in collaborative discussions
- Present ideas clearly
- Respond thoughtfully to questions
- Adapt speech to context and audience

Teach Like Ced™ Alignment

Daily Oral Language Integration
- Turn-and-talks
- Structured discussions
- Think-alouds

Formal Oral Presentations
- Short, focused, standards-aligned
- Emphasize clarity, organization, and reasoning

Academic Language Stems
- Support respectful discourse
- Promote evidence-based communication

Result: Speaking is treated as literacy—not a soft skill.

4. Language Standards Alignment

Core Language Expectations

Students are expected to:
- Use conventions correctly
- Apply vocabulary accurately
- Understand how language functions

Teach Like Ced™ Alignment

Language in Context
- Grammar taught through writing, not worksheets
- Vocabulary embedded in authentic expression

Revision as Language Practice
- Students refine word choice intentionally
- Mechanics serve meaning, not the reverse

Result: Language standards are applied meaningfully—not memorized.

5. Integration of Knowledge & Ideas

Standards Expectation

Students are expected to:
- Synthesize information
- Evaluate ideas
- Express understanding across formats

Teach Like Ced™ Alignment

Writing + Speaking Integration
- Students write, speak, revise, and reflect
- Knowledge is demonstrated in multiple modalities

Cumulative Mastery
- Skills build intentionally across units
- Learning transfers across tasks

Result: Students move from surface understanding to **ownership of knowledge**.

6. Differentiation Within Standards

Teach Like Ced™ aligns with standards while recognizing learner variability.

Differentiation occurs through:
- Scaffolding
- Pacing
- Support structures

—not through lowered expectations.

Result: All students access grade-level standards with integrity.

7. Alignment Across Grade Bands

Teach Like Ced™ is vertically aligned.

The framework:
- Scales across grade levels
- Adjusts complexity, not structure
- Builds coherence across classrooms and schools

Result: Literacy instruction becomes **systemic**, not fragmented.

Conclusion: Standards Achieved Through Clarity, Not Compliance

Teach Like Ced™ proves that standards are best met when:
- Instruction is intentional
- Structure is explicit
- Culture is honored
- Voice is required

This crosswalk confirms that Teach Like Ced™ is not an alternative to standards-based instruction—it is a **powerful implementation model** for achieving it with depth, equity, and sustainability.

APPENDIX C

Sample Lesson Walkthrough: Sentence → Paragraph → Presentation

Teach Like Ced™ Educator Handbook

Cedric A. Washington
Who Lives Like This?! Publishing LLC

Purpose of This Walkthrough

This sample lesson walkthrough demonstrates how Teach Like Ced™ operates during a real instructional cycle. It shows how:
- Structure drives clarity
- Writing builds comprehension
- Oral language reinforces confidence
- SELF is embedded naturally

This is not a "perfect lesson."
It is a **replicable lesson**.

Lesson Overview

Grade Band: Middle School (adaptable across grades)
Literacy Focus: Opinion Writing / Explanation
Text Type: Short informational or narrative passage
Framework Components Used:
- Sentence → Paragraph → Presentation
- Monday–Friday Instructional Flow
- Oral Language Integration
- Student Workbook Use
- SELF Integration

Instructional Objective

Students will:
- Write a clear sentence stating an opinion or claim
- Develop the idea into a structured paragraph
- Present their thinking orally using academic language

MONDAY: Modeling the Sentence (Teacher-Led)

Teacher Focus:

- Modeling thinking aloud
- Demonstrating sentence structure
- Normalizing revision

Teacher Language (Example):

"I'm going to write a sentence that tells what I believe and why. I'm not worried about being perfect—I'm focused on being clear."

Teacher writes:

I believe education is important because it helps people create opportunities.

Teacher then revises aloud:

"I want to be more specific. Let me try again."

Revised sentence:

I believe education is important because it helps people gain opportunities they might not otherwise have.

Student Action:
- Students listen
- Students discuss what makes the sentence clear
- Students identify the claim and reason

Workbook Use:
- Students highlight the claim
- Students underline the reason

TUESDAY: Oral Rehearsal & Guided Practice

Teacher Focus:
- Oral language
- Sentence rehearsal
- Academic language coaching

Teacher Prompt:

"Turn to a partner and say your sentence out loud using the frame:
I believe ___ because ___."

Teacher circulates and coaches:
- Clarifying vague language
- Encouraging complete thoughts

Student Action:
- Students rehearse sentences orally

- Students revise ideas verbally before writing

Workbook Use:
- Students write their sentence
- Sentence frames are provided as support

WEDNESDAY: Paragraph Development

Teacher Focus:
- Expanding ideas
- Maintaining structure

Teacher Modeling:

Teacher shows how one sentence grows into a paragraph:
1. Claim sentence
2. Example or evidence
3. Explanation
4. Closing thought

Student Action:
- Students expand their sentence into a paragraph
- Teachers confer individually

Workbook Use:
- Paragraph organizer guides development
- Students label each part

THURSDAY: Revision & Dialogue

Teacher Focus:
- Revision as ownership
- Peer discussion

Teacher Prompt:

"Read your paragraph and ask yourself:
Is my idea clear to someone else?"

Peer discussion questions:
- What part was strongest?
- Where could it be clearer?

Student Action:
- Students revise for clarity
- Students explain revisions orally

Workbook Use:
- Students make visible edits
- Reflection question included

FRIDAY: Presentation & Reflection

Teacher Focus:
- Voice
- Confidence
- Application

Student Presentations:
- Students present their paragraph orally
- Use academic language stems

Example stem:

I believe ___ because ___. One example is ___.

Assessment:
- Clarity
- Organization
- Confidence

Reflection Prompt:

"How did your thinking improve this week?"

Workbook Use:
- Students write reflection
- Growth is documented

How SELF Is Embedded Throughout
- **SELF Conscience:** Students own ideas
- **SELF Governing:** Students revise intentionally
- **Social Conscience:** Students consider audience
- **Aspirations:** Writing connects to purpose
- **Good People Skills:** Students listen and respond respectfully

SELF is not a separate lesson—it is **lived through literacy**.

Differentiation Within the Lesson
- Sentence frames support struggling writers
- Oral rehearsal supports language development
- Extended paragraphs challenge advanced learners

All students engage with the same core task.

What This Walkthrough Demonstrates

This lesson shows that Teach Like Ced™:
- Is structured, not rigid
- Is culturally intelligent, not controversial
- Is rigorous, not overwhelming
- Is empowering, not permissive

Conclusion: From Theory to Practice

This walkthrough illustrates how Teach Like Ced™ moves seamlessly from:
- Sentence
- To paragraph
- To voice

This is literacy instruction that builds thinkers—**on purpose**.

APPENDIX D

Family Engagement as Cultural Partnership

Teach Like Ced™ Educator Handbook

Cedric A. Washington
Who Lives Like This?! Publishing LLC

Purpose of This Appendix

Family engagement is often treated as an afterthought in literacy instruction—limited to newsletters, conferences, or homework reminders.

Teach Like Ced™ challenges that model.

This appendix establishes a guiding principle:

> **Families are not supplemental to literacy development. They are foundational to it.**

Students 'first literacy experiences do not occur in classrooms. They occur at home, in community, through conversation, storytelling, observation, and lived experience.

Teach Like Ced™ recognizes families as **co-educators**, not spectators.

Why Traditional Family Engagement Often Falls Short

Conventional family engagement strategies frequently:
- Assume deficit perspectives
- Prioritize compliance over connection
- Communicate *at* families instead of *with* them

Examples include:
- "Help your child with homework" without guidance
- One-way communication filled with academic jargon
- Expectations disconnected from family realities

These approaches unintentionally alienate families and limit impact.

Teach Like Ced™ replaces this with **partnership grounded in respect**.

Culture Begins at Home

Families shape:
- Language patterns
- Storytelling traditions
- Communication norms
- Values around learning

Teach Like Ced™ acknowledges that culture is transmitted first in the home, not the school.

Instead of attempting to replace these influences, the framework seeks to **align with them**.

When home and school operate in harmony, literacy accelerates.

Redefining Family Engagement Through Literacy

Teach Like Ced™ frames family engagement around **language and thinking**, not assignments.

Families are encouraged to:
- Talk with students about ideas
- Ask "why" and "how" questions
- Listen to explanations
- Validate effort and growth

Families do not need advanced academic knowledge to support literacy.
They need **clarity and access**.

Accessible Literacy Practices for Families

Teach Like Ced™ equips families with simple, powerful practices:

1. Conversation as Literacy

Encourage families to ask:
- "What did you write about today?"
- "What do you believe and why?"
- "Explain your thinking to me."

These conversations reinforce reasoning and clarity.

2. Oral Rehearsal at Home

Students may practice:
- Explaining sentences aloud
- Summarizing ideas verbally
- Rehearsing presentations

Speaking strengthens confidence and comprehension.

3. Celebrating Growth, Not Perfection

Families are encouraged to:
- Praise effort
- Notice improvement
- Normalize revision

This aligns home support with classroom philosophy.

Removing Barriers to Engagement

Teach Like Ced™ recognizes common barriers:
- Time constraints
- Language differences
- Past negative school experiences

The framework promotes:
- Clear communication
- Respectful tone
- Multiple access points (oral, written, visual)

Engagement is designed to be **inclusive**, not exclusive.

Honoring Family Knowledge and Voice

Families possess knowledge that schools do not:
- Cultural history
- Community wisdom
- Lived experience

Teach Like Ced™ encourages educators to:
- Listen to families
- Invite perspectives
- Respect insights

This mutual respect strengthens trust and collaboration.

Family Engagement Without Overburdening

Teach Like Ced™ does not ask families to:
- Become teachers
- Replicate classroom instruction
- Manage complex assignments

Instead, families are invited to:
- Encourage thinking
- Ask questions
- Affirm student voice

Small actions produce meaningful impact.

Supporting Multigenerational Literacy

Teach Like Ced™ views literacy as intergenerational.

Students often:
- Explain school learning to siblings
- Share ideas with caregivers
- Model language for younger children

This creates a ripple effect—literacy extends beyond the individual student.

The Educator's Role in Building Partnership

Educators are responsible for:
- Communicating clearly
- Inviting collaboration
- Avoiding deficit language
- Valuing family contributions

Teach Like Ced™ classrooms operate with the understanding that:

Trust accelerates learning.

What Family Engagement Is Not

To maintain clarity, Teach Like Ced™ defines what engagement is not.

It is not:
- Monitoring compliance
- Policing homework
- Judging home environments

It is:
- Encouraging dialogue
- Supporting growth
- Strengthening identity

Conclusion: Literacy as a Shared Responsibility

Teach Like Ced™ affirms that literacy is not confined to classrooms.

It lives in:
- Conversations
- Stories
- Questions
- Explanations

When families and educators partner through culture, language, and respect, students experience literacy as **belonging**, not pressure.

This appendix completes the Teach Like Ced™ Educator Handbook by extending its impact from the classroom into the community—where literacy truly lives.